Sliceforms

John Sharp

Mathema
pap

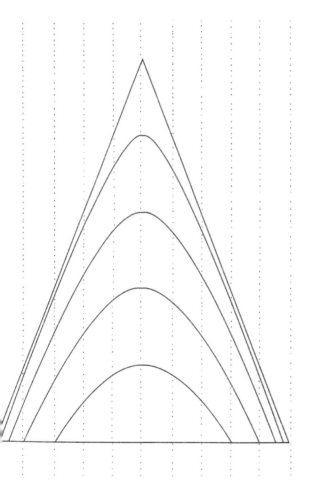

Tarquin Publications

What are Sliceforms?

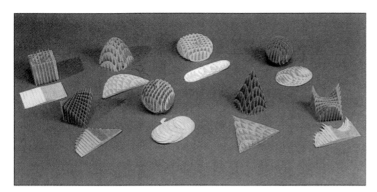

Pictures of sliceform models do not show their full beauty. Only by making and physically handling the models can their true dynamic qualities be fully appreciated. Their three-dimensional forms and surfaces are defined or suggested by two intersecting sets of parallel slices. These intersections act as a multitude of hinges and as a consequence each model can be made to collapse flat in two different ways. Between these two extreme positions the surface passes through a host of different but related shapes. By using different colours for the slices in each direction, the patterns generated as the model is manipulated can be very attractive and unexpected.

Most sliceform models are designed so that when the sets of slices are at right angles the surface that they define takes up its desired form, usually a symmetrical one. The majority of the surfaces which make the most attractive sliceform models have a high degree of symmetry. Of course this symmetry also ensures that many slices are similar or indeed identical and so the time that it takes to draw all the slices is correspondingly reduced.

Six of the eight sliceforms in this book are closed shapes which can be modelled with two perpendicular planes of symmetry. The other two, and some people consider that they are in fact even more attractive, are carefully chosen sections from particular infinite three-dimensional surfaces. The monkey saddle model has only a single plane of symmetry and therefore only four pairs of slices are identical. The conoid surface model lacks any planes of symmetry and so all eighteen slices are different.

Being built of thin slices, the volume of the model has little actual substance and the views into the interior and the interplay of the colours and shadows give them an almost magical quality.

In contrast with what could be called 'normal' mathematical models, no part of the surface is ever represented by flat p… The surface is always suggested by the edges of the slices. Sometimes, surprisingly little of the actual surface being modelled is actually there and yet this illusion undoubtedly adds to the general attractiveness of the models.

Although models made from slices have a long history, the potential has not been fully realised. It is hoped that this will act as a starting point for a mathematical and artistic exploration of some of the possibilities which the sliceform method offers. You do not need to have a mathematical background to make these models or indeed to design original sliceforms of your own. Just a sense of three-dimensional space. Undoubtedly a study and investigation of sliceform models is an excellent means of developing just such a sense

Additionally, if you have a good understanding of both computers and co-ordinate geometry, you can set out to acquire the technique of programming a computer to produce the slices directly from the equation of the surface. This is demanding process, but it opens the door to the discovery new surfaces which would make interesting sliceform mod…

Even without any knowledge of programming at all, you would find that a computer is a great help. It can be used simply as a drawing tool. Within a drawing package it is e… to duplicate slices and it is then a simple matter to print o… complete set on to any suitably coloured sheet of paper. If have access to a scanner, then the half-size plans inside th… back cover can be scanned in and modified to generate fur… versions of the eight models in this book.

Making the models

‍ting

se one of the models and remove the relevant pages from
ook. Cut precisely round the outline of each slice and its
The tabs are cut away when the model is assembled, so do
ut them off yet. They are needed to keep track of which
is which.

ust into the colour so that no white shows. Do not cut too
The outline of the colour is the exact shape you need.

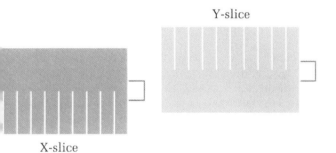

Y-slice

X-slice

lots are definitely slots and not simple cuts. Cut along
sides of each of the slots so that no white remains but no
er into the colour than that. Carefully remove the
ting slivers of paper. In this book, all the X-slices have
slots coming from the bottom and the Y-slices from the
nd each corresponding pair meets exactly at their mid-
s.

up one model completely before starting to cut out
er. The actual finished width of the slots after you have
em out is very important. Erring on the thin side when
g slots is better than cutting them too wide; you can
s cut more off, but you can never put it back. If your first
l seems a little too tight or too loose, then you can modify
you cut the slots on the next one.

‍embling

ge all the slices into numerical order. You will see that
ntral X-slice has its tab coloured red. This is the one to
with whichever method of assembly you use.

Method 1

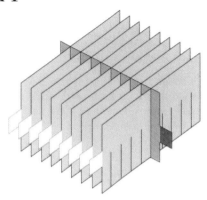

Place all the Y-slices into the central X-slice at their middle
slots. Then turn the whole model over and add one Y-slice at
a time, working outwards from the centre.

Method 2

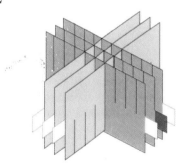

Place only the central three Y-slices into the central X-slice
and then turn over. Then add the corresponding X-slice to
either side of the central one, giving three slices in each
direction which meet at nine places. Complete the model by
adding X and Y slices alternately, working outwards from this
central group.

Whatever emotions you may feel if a piece you have just put in
drops out as you try to put in the next, do persevere. It gets
easier as you continue and the finished models are so
beautiful!

Sliceforms

How to design models of your own

The slices which define the surface or object are spaced at regular distances in two directions, usually two directions at right angles. Each slice has to be of exactly the correct shape and size to generate the required surface.

The technique of sliceform modelling is really the search for methods of working out how to draw each of the slices correctly. A simple model of a cube is a good one to start with and to explain the method of working.

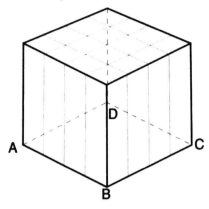

The diagram above shows a cube and how it could be sliced into quarters in two directions at right angles. It is clear that all the slices will be identical and that each is a square.

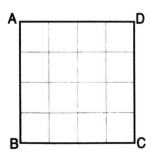

The plan view would look like this. All the lines on the grid are potential slices, but the four edges of the base, AB, BC, CD and DA cannot be used for the model. They do not intersect with any other slices and therefore would have no support.

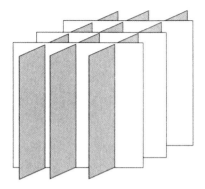

This cube would then be modelled by only three slices in ⬦ direction. While this number is sufficient to demonstrate ⬦ principle, it is not enough to make a really pleasing model The cut-out model on pages 7-10 is based on this way of representing the cube but with seven slices each way. Wit symmetrical models an odd number of slices gives a better result than an even number. The central slice then forms ⬦ plane of symmetry. Generally, it is best to settle on either seven or nine slices in each direction.

The convention used in this book is that slots are cut from base in the X direction and from the top in the Y direction theory, it is only necessary that the lengths of the pairs of ⬦ add up to the depth of the model at the line of intersection it is far simpler to cut exactly to the mid-point on each. T⬦ frustration of having to sort out problems caused by slot le⬦ errors makes it just not worth the effort of trying to be original! Let all slices meet at their mid-points.

A cube represented in this way has a well-defined surface its top and bottom faces, but the side faces are more imagi⬦ than real and the four vertical edges of the cube do not exi⬦ all. It is an attractive feature of sliceform models that simi⬦ faces often have different surface treatments. This differer⬦ is sharper in models where surfaces are flat rather than cu⬦ but the effect is always there if you look for it.

delling a right cone

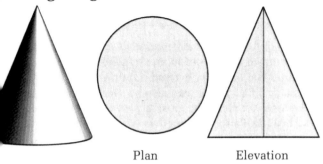

Plan   Elevation

ht cone is one where the base is at right angles to the axis
t is a good model to use to illustrate how to determine the
es of curved slices. This example has only five slices each
and not the nine of the cut-out model on pages 11-14.
ever, the principle is the same.

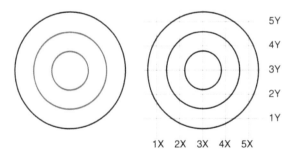

1X   2X   3X   4X   5X

base is a circle so draw it first. Then add the two smaller
es which correspond to the two evenly spaced cross
ons, shown in red on the elevation view above.

draw a symmetrically placed square grid over the plan.
line on this grid corresponds to a vertical slice through
one. Each slice is therefore parallel to the axis and is
endicular to the base.

central slices 3X and 3Y are isosceles triangles and must
entical to the elevation view. The other slices are parallel
e axis and you may remember from your knowledge of
sections that each will be a hyperbola.

However, it is not necessary to know what a hyperbola is in
order to be able to construct it. Its shape is obtained point by
point by drawing and transferring distances from the plan.

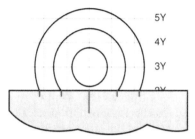

To draw slice 2Y, place a straight-edged piece of paper along
line 2Y on the plan and mark the central line and where the
circles cross the edge.

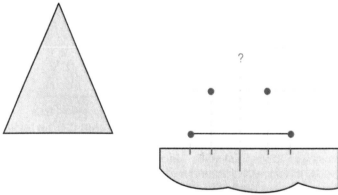

Draw the elevation view and project horizontal lines from the
base and where the cone has the radius of each of the two
innermost circles. Use the paper edge to mark the central line
and the points corresponding to intersections of the base and
the middle circle. This establishes four points which lie on
the outline of the slice.

From the plan you can see that slice 2Y does not intersect the
smallest circle. It is therefore certain that on the elevation it
does not reach up as far as the corresponding horizontal line.
To draw the slice correctly, it is necessary to plot its highest
point. That is the next problem to solve!

Sliceforms

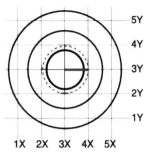

The dotted circle has been drawn to touch slice 2Y. Its radius is therefore the radius of the cross section of the cone at the highest point of the slice.

On the elevation view, establish where the cone has that radius and then project a line horizontally from it. The highest point of the slice is reached at the point where this line meets the central line of the slice. Once five points are plotted, they can be joined with a smooth curve to give the outline of the slice. This has been achieved without ever being aware that its shape is a hyperbola!

If five points are not enough to give a smooth enough curve, simply draw more circles on the base corresponding to different heights on the side view and repeat the procedure.

The shape for slice 2Y will also serve for slices 2X, 4Y & 4X. Slice 1Y can be constructed using a similar method and it will then serve for slices 5Y, 1X & 5X as well.

Using combinations of this method and the one on page 4, you can make many different types of model. Try recreating other models in this book to test that the methods are understood.

What kind of paper or card should be us

This book has been printed on crisp white cartridge paper a the colours for the models have been printed on to the surf

If you wish to make sliceform models of your own, a good of thin card to use is sold in art supplies shops. This come a variety of colours and is dyed right through. It may be 140gsm or 160gsm, but may also be available in a rather thicker and heavier form, possibly up to 200gsm. You can make beautiful sliceform models with all these weights of but you will need to test how wide to make the slots. Whe the slot width is correct, the model collapses cleanly in bot directions but the slices do not easily fall out.

If you want to make models which are rather larger, the car will certainly need to be thicker and more rigid. The amou of card and number of slices required can sometimes be deceptive but it is possible to use the models in the book a guide and scale up the size.

Further templates are provided on the inside cover of this b

Further Reading

Since this book was originally published, a more detailed exploration of how sliceforms can be used to explore surfac has been produced by Tarquin Publications. *Surfaces*: *Explorations with Sliceforms* provides the reader with the techniques to produce sliceform models of any object. It examines in turn the particular methodologies required f different types of geometrical form, concluding with commentary on software available and some additional tem

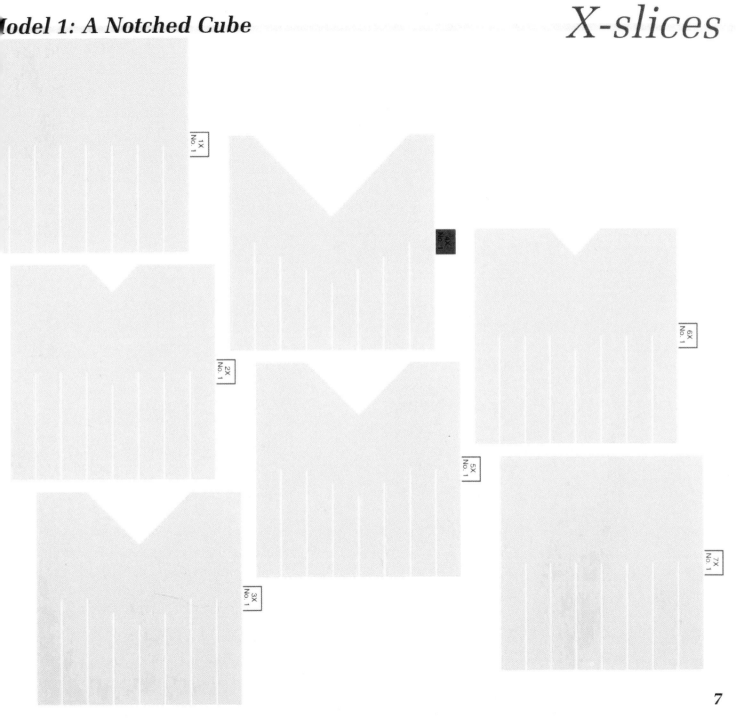

1X
No. 1

2X
No. 1

3X
No. 1

4X
No. 1

5X
No. 1

6X
No. 1

7X
No. 1

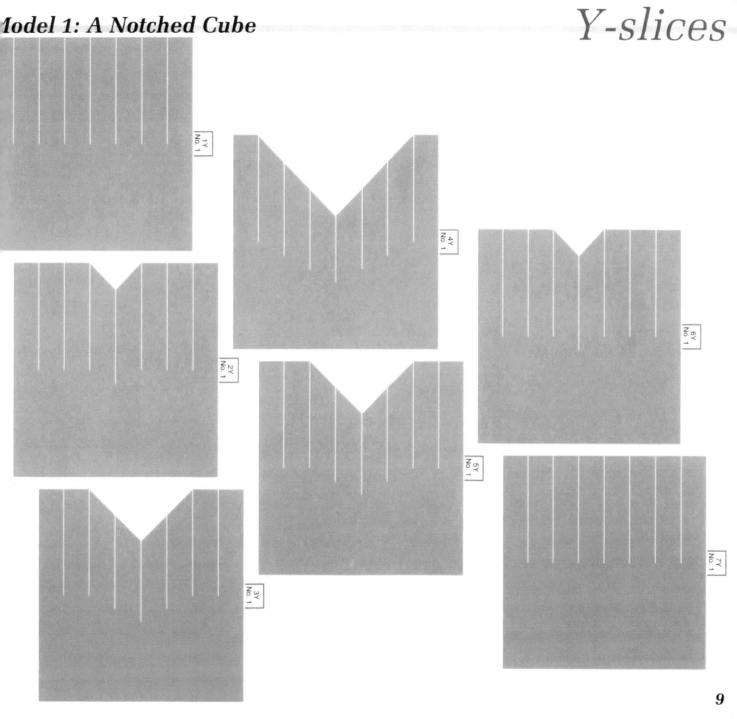

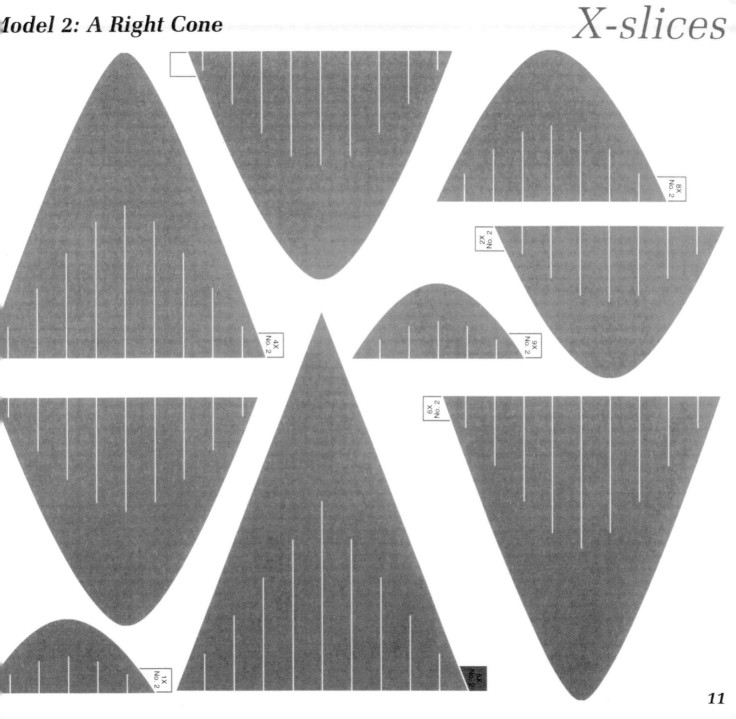

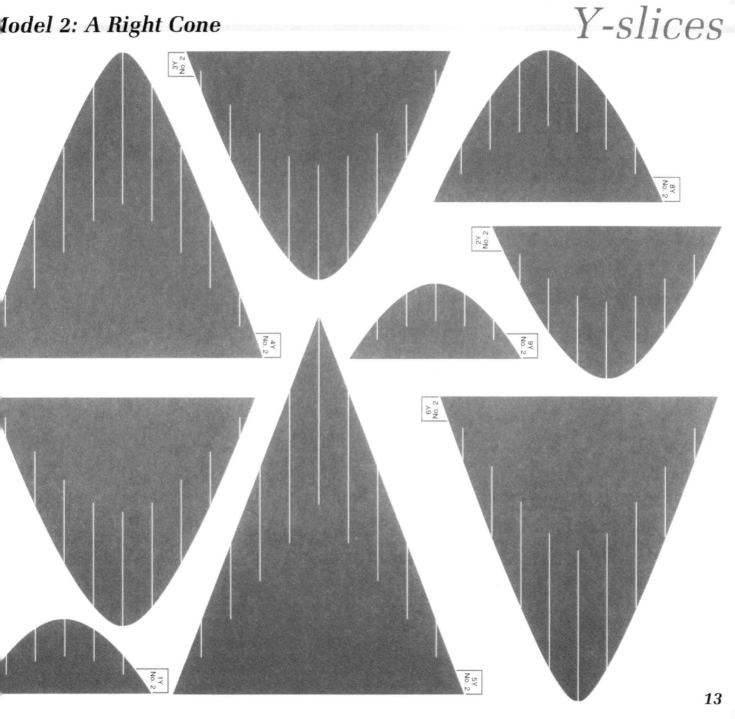

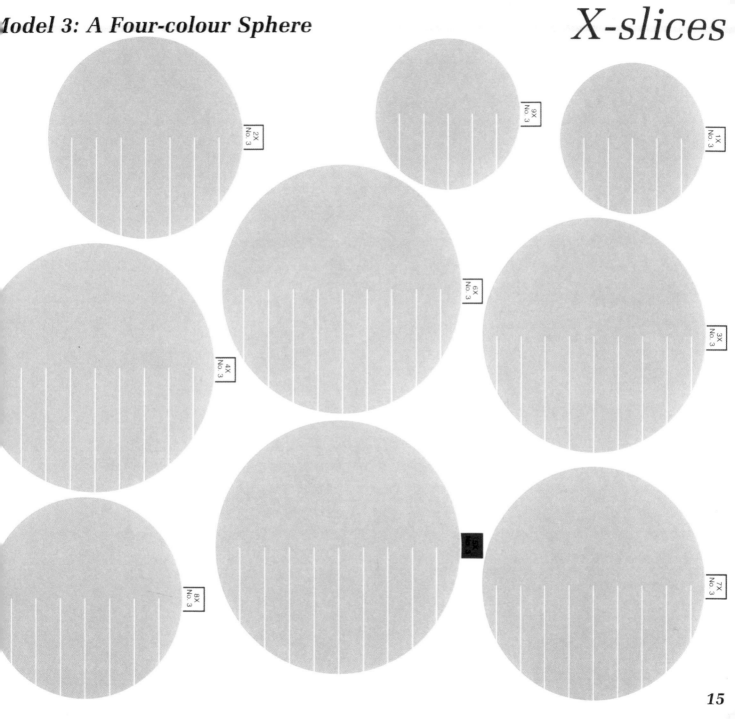

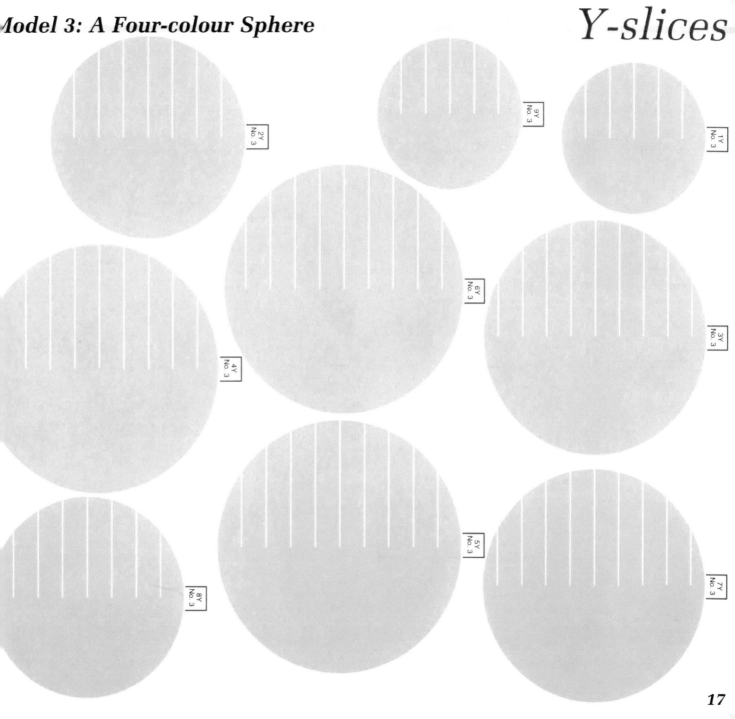

2Y
No. 3

9Y
No. 3

1Y
No. 3

6Y
No. 3

4Y
No. 3

3Y
No. 3

5Y
No. 3

8Y
No. 3

7Y
No. 3

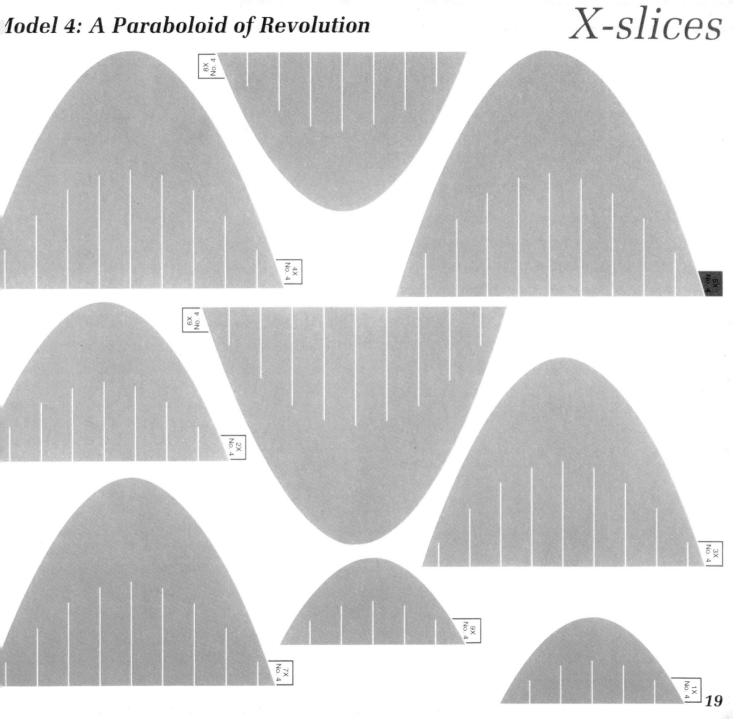

8X
No. 4

4X
No. 4

5X
No. 4

6X
No. 4

2X
No. 4

3X
No. 4

7X
No. 4

9X
No. 4

1X
No. 4

Model 4: A Paraboloid of Revolution

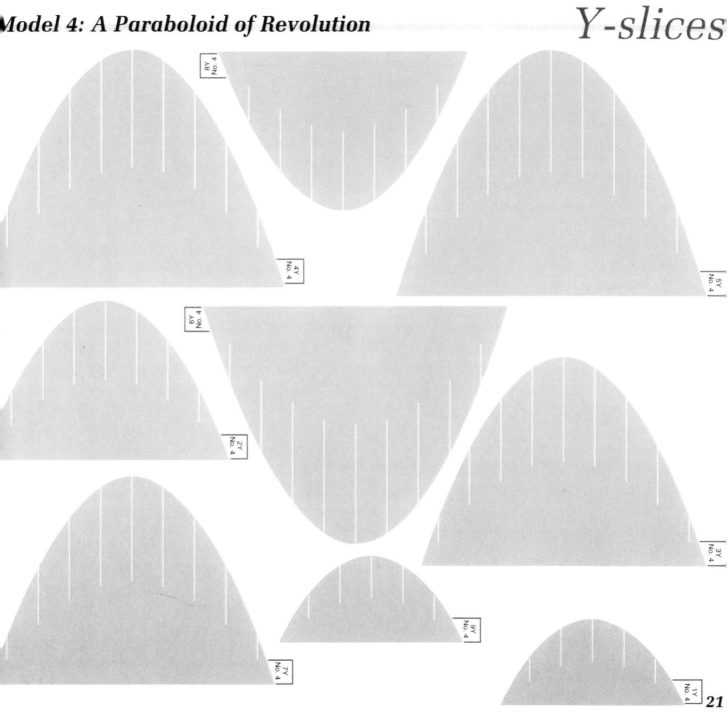

8Y No. 4

4Y No. 4

5Y No. 4

6Y No. 4

2Y No. 4

3Y No. 4

7Y No. 4

9Y No. 4

1Y No. 4

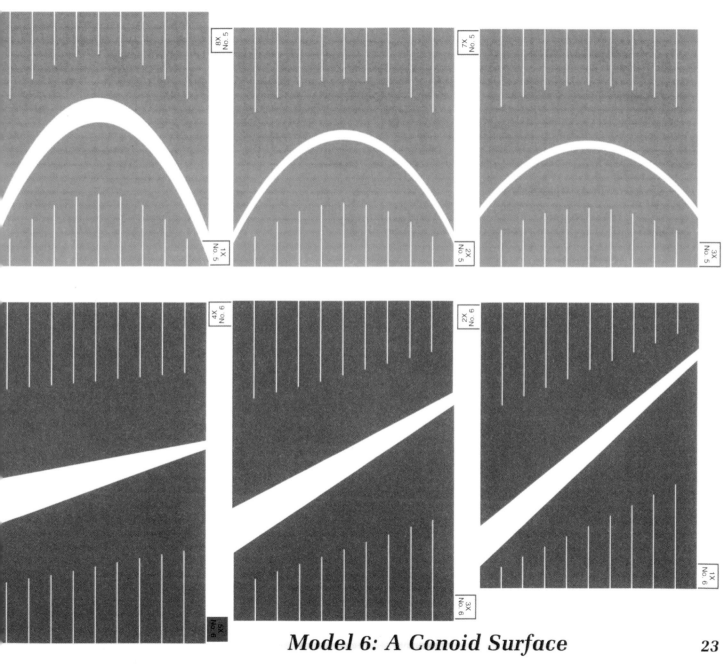

8X No. 5

7X No. 5

1X No. 5

2X No. 5

3X No. 5

4X No. 6

2X No. 6

5X No. 6

3X No. 6

1X No. 6

Model 6: A Conoid Surface

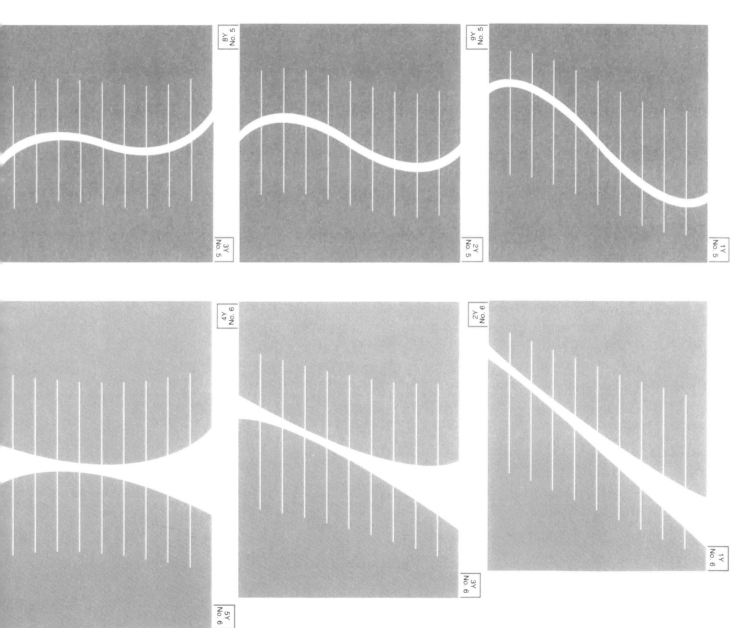

6X
No. 5

5Y
No. 5

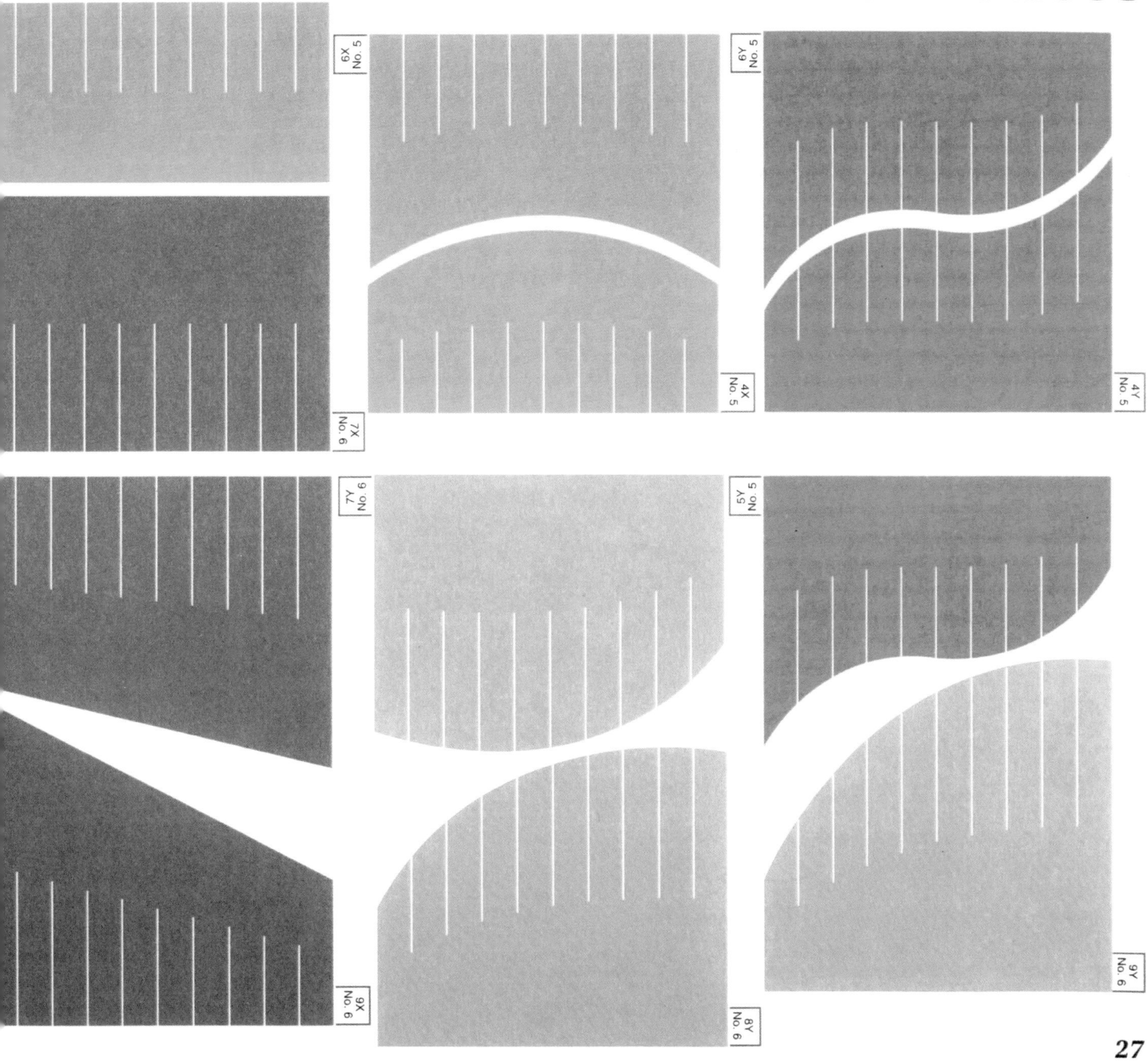

7X
No. 5

4X
No. 5

4Y
No. 5

7Y
No. 6

5Y
No. 5

6X
No. 6

8Y
No. 6

9Y
No. 6

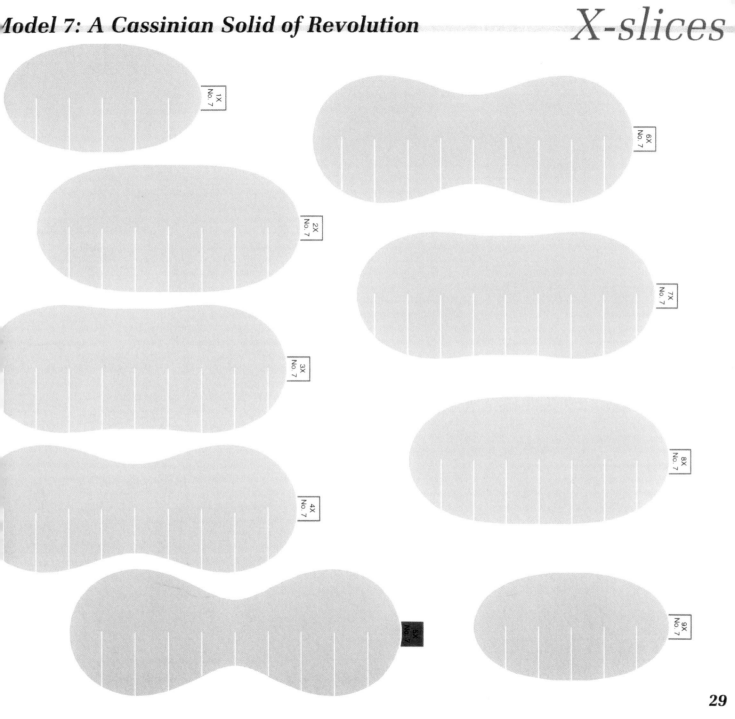

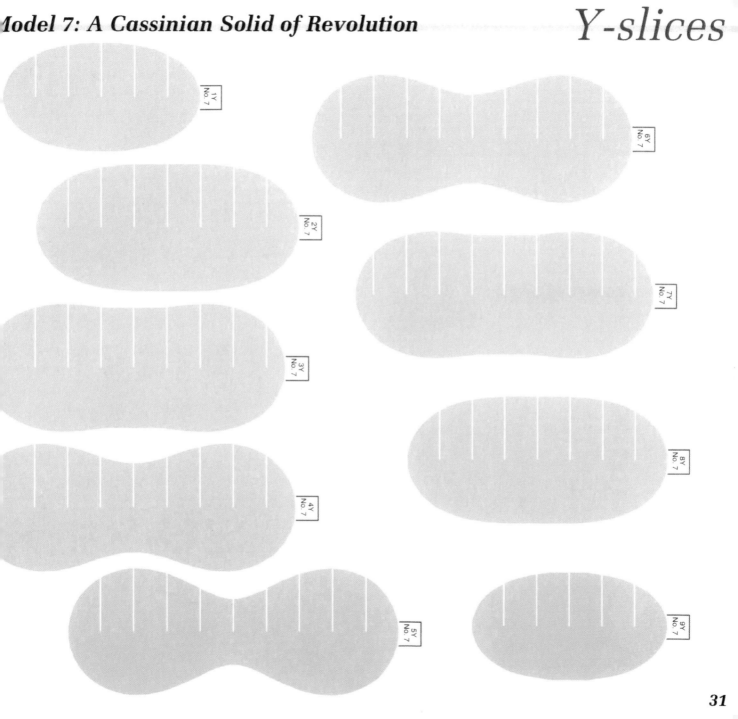

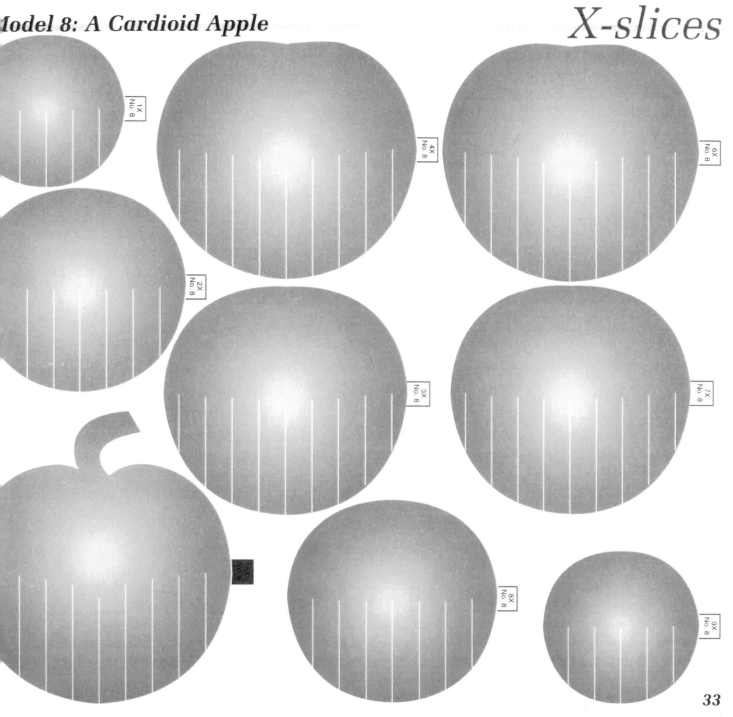

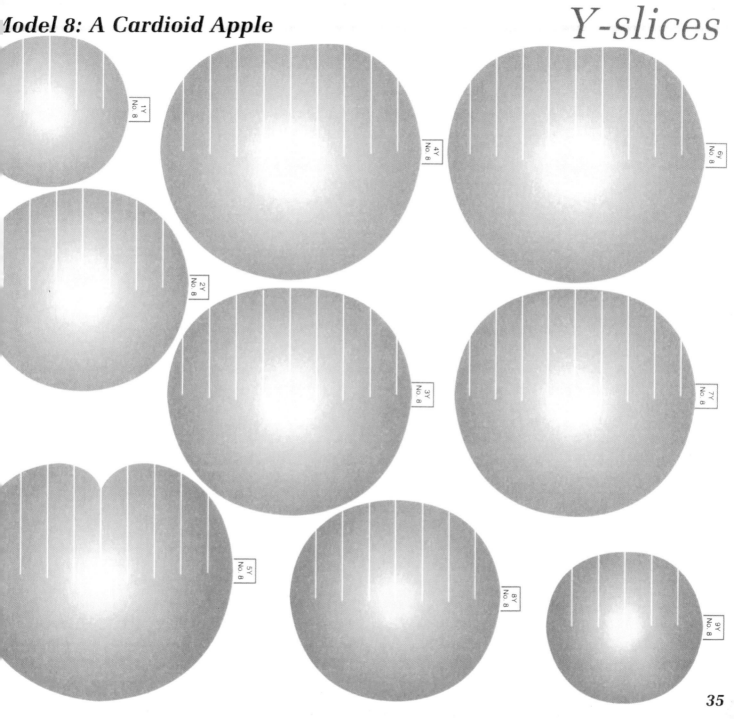

1Y
No. 8

2Y
No. 8

3Y
No. 8

4Y
No. 8

5Y
No. 8

6Y
No. 8

7Y
No. 8

8Y
No. 8

9Y
No. 8